Dear mouse friends,
Welcome to the world of

Geronimo Stilton

The Rodent's Gazette
Editorial Staff

Geronimo Stilton
A learned and brainy mouse; editor of *The Rodent's Gazette*

Thea Stilton
Geronimo's sister and special correspondent at *The Rodent's Gazette*

Trap Stilton
An awful joker; Geronimo's cousin and owner of the store Cheap Junk for Less

Benjamin Stilton
A sweet and loving nine-year-old mouse; Geronimo's favorite nephew

Geronimo Stilton

THE LAST RESORT OASIS

Scholastic Inc.

Published by Scholastic Inc., *Publishers since 1920,* 557 Broadway, New York, NY 10012. SCHOLASTIC and associated logos are trademarks and/or registered trademarks of Scholastic Inc.

ISBN 978-93-90590-38-4

Text by Geronimo Stilton

Original title *Vacanze da sogno all'Oasi Sputacchiosa*
Cover by Iacopo Bruno, Roberto Ronchi, and Alessandro Muscillo
Illustrations by Danilo Loizedda, Carolina Livio, Daria Cerchi, and Valeria Cairoli
Translated by Anna Pizzelli
Special thanks to Shannon Penney
Interior design by Becky James

Printed in India at Sai Printo Pack Pvt. Ltd.
First printing 2021
This reprint edition August 2025

A Busy Night

It was a chilly winter night in New Mouse City, and I was still in my office. From the window, I could see **snowflakes** falling. Holey cheese, it looked like the city was slowly being covered with fluffy **whipped cream** . . .

What an **INCREDIMOUSE** view!

Oh, wait! Silly me, I haven't introduced myself . . .

My name is Stilton, *Geronimo Stilton*,

and I am the publisher and editor in chief of *The Rodent's Gazette*, the most famouse newspaper on Mouse Island.

As I was saying, it was a chilly winter night and I was just finishing a very busy day of work. I had:

written **10** articles,

edited **20** manuscripts,

made **30** phone calls, and

received **40** phone calls.

Chattering cheddar, being in charge of a newspaper is hard work!

I was tired, worn out, exhausted!

But just as I was finally about to put on my jacket and leave for vacation . . .

Knock, Knock!

Rotten ricotta, who could that be?!

The door opened, and one of our staff writers, Babs Bonbon, poked her snout into my office. "Mr. Stilton, I'm about to go, but I'm leaving you my latest article to review. It needs to go to press right away for the special edition. Have a good vacation, and thank you!"

"B-but, actually . . . I was just about to . . ." I stuttered in surprise.

Before I could continue, I noticed some other **reportermice** in line behind Babs Bonbon: Jim Dribbles, Vanessa Vogue, and Cara DeColores.

"Here's my article on **WORKOUT** regimes to keep fit during the winter!"

"And my special on cold-weather fashion!"

"And here's the cover article!"

HOLEY CHEESE, I had forgotten that I still needed to go through the whole SPECIAL EDITION!

After my colleagues left, my DESK was swamped. And I had thought I was ready to start my vacation! I sighed, took my jacket off, and got back to work.

Why, oh why, does everything always happen to me?

Snow in New Mouse City

After what seemed like forever, I finished reading the last article: "Ten Ways to Make the Perfect **Snowman**." I rubbed my snout with exhaustion and squeaked out loud, "Oh, I wish I were home in my comfy armchair!"

Just then a sound broke the silence in the quiet newsroom.

RING!

I nearly jumped out of my fur and then picked up the phone.

A familiar voice hollering on the other end of the line made me **jump** out of my fur all over again. "Grandson, what are you still doing there? Don't you know what time it is?"

It was my grandfather, **William Shortpaws**! "Actually, I was just finishing up," I started to explain.

"No excuses, Grandson!" he hollered. "You are not going to miss tonight's family dinner! **Let's go, let's go, let's go!**"

I looked up at the clock.

Moldy mozzarella, it was already seven thirty and we were supposed to have dinner at Aunt Sweetfur's house at eight! I only had half an hour to get there, and I wanted to bring **GIFTS** for my niece Trappy and nephew Benjamin.

As fast as a rat with a cat on his tail, I hung

up the phone, sent all the articles to the printer, and squeaked, "I'M COMING!"

I scurried to the coatrack and put on my jacket, scarf, and wool hat. As soon as I stepped out of the office, I shivered from the ends of my whiskers to the tip of my tail.

"It's freezing!" I yelped.

I took a deep breath and glanced around. New Mouse City looked so beautiful! Its streets were crowded with smiling rodents, and the twinkling STREETLIGHTS were reflected in the snow.

Even though it was cold, I couldn't resist WALKING through that beautiful winter wonderland. But I didn't have much time. I had to get my tail in gear!

I headed downtown, but when I turned the CORNER . . .

SPLAT!

A snowball hit me in the back of the head! **Thundering cattails!** I had walked right through a group of **mouselets** having a snowball fight!

One of them squeaked, "Oops, sorry, sir! That was an accident!"

I **turned** toward him to say, "Oh, it's oka —"

But I wasn't watching where I was walking, so I tripped.

WHOOSH!

I went tail over snout and landed on the ground with a thud.

RATS, that hurt!

As if that wasn't bad enough, I was still sliding on the icy snow, faster and faster. I couldn't stop!

Until I slammed into a store window.

Why, oh why, does everything always happen to me?

I shook my snout and then noticed that I had hit the window of a travel agency called the Traveling Rodent. A poster read:

GET AWAY TO SOMEPLACE WARM!

I looked at the poster more closely. It was an ad for a trip to the Black Jungle. Ooh, too **DANGEROUS**! After all, I'm a bit of a 'fraidy mouse.

There was another poster for a cruise on the Ratatlantic Ocean. Ugh, too bad I get **seasick**!

Then there was one more, for a trip to Bald Island. The blue sky and sunshine there looked fabumouse. But I really don't like to **fly**!

No, I was happy to stay right here in New

Mouse City, no matter how cold it was!

In the window there were also two photography **BOOKS**, featuring the warmest and coldest locations on Mouse Island.

"There!" I cried, excited. "Those are perfect gifts for my beloved Benjamin and Trappy!"

A Special Gift

By the time I arrived at Aunt Sweetfur's house, I was tired, out of breath, and as cold as a mozzarella milkshake!

I rang the bell, and a few moments later, Aunt Sweetfur opened the door. When she saw me, she gave me a big hug. Ah, she smelled like lavender, as always. "Come on in, it's **warm** inside!" she said, opening the door wide.

I really loved Aunt Sweetfur's house. I had

so many mousetastic memories there! After all, I had been brought up in that house, along with my sister, THEA, and my cousin Trap.

Suddenly, someone squeaked, "Welcome, Uncle G!"

Benjamin ran over to me, arms open wide. Trappy was right behind him, calling, "You're finally here!"

After greeting my niece and nephew, I took off my jacket and Aunt Sweetfur led me to the dining room. It was a Stilton tradition to have family dinners there. The table was covered with whisker-licking good food. YUM!

Grandfather William's voice boomed, "There you are, Grandson! One more minute and I was going to take *The Rodent's Gazette* back from you!"

Rancid ricotta, my grandfather sure knew how to make a point!

With a little smile, he added, "I'm happy that you're here."

"We're all finally here!" Thea, Trap, and Uncle Grayfur squeaked, clapping their paws.

I had to admit, I was touched! (After all, my heart is as soft as mascarpone cheese.)

It was so nice to be together with my whole family.

We sat down to eat, and after a fabumouse dinner, my family said they had a surprise for me. My vacation week was really starting off on the right paw!

"This is the anniversary of the time you took over at *The Rodent's Gazette*!" Thea said, pawing me a gift. "Come on, shake a tail and open it!"

I was as curious as a cat! I opened the box and — **holey cheese**, what was it?

Thea explained, "Those are **SNOWSHOES**. You use them to walk on the snow! Now you can exercise in the winter."

My dear readers, you know that I am not

an **ATHLETIC** mouse! But Thea's gift was so thoughtful, I smiled and said, "Thank you, Thea! I love them."

Next was a gift from Trap. I unwrapped it, and . . .

BOOOOOM!

Confetti went flying into the air!

How scary!

I was shaking from the ends of my whiskers to the tip of my tail.

Trappy exclaimed, "Cheese and crackers! That was a great **PRANK**, Uncle Trap!"

My cousin smiled. "Thanks! What about you, CousinKins, did you like my prank?" Cheese niblets, Trap will never change!

But before I had a chance to reply, Grandfather William cleared his throat, grabbed a large yellow envelope, and said: "And here is my gift, Grandson. It's really for the whole family!"

I could see that everyone was very curious. What could be inside?

Grandfather William OPENED the envelope and handed it to Trappy, who read out loud: "You are all invited on a Stilton family vacation. Departure is set for . . . tomorrow morning!"

Aunt Sweetfur and Uncle Grayfur had big smiles on their snouts. "We told Grandfather William that we've already booked a romantic cruise. But have a great trip!"

Trap cried, "I can't wait!"

"Mouserific, a real vacation!" Thea squeaked.

Benjamin and Trappy were jumping up and down with joy.

I was the only one who asked, "But where are we going?"

Grandfather William looked at me for a moment, and then replied, "No questions, Grandson! It's a surprise!"

Holey cheese, where was he going to take us? This smelled like trouble!

Beep — Beeeeep!

The following morning at dawn, I heard a very loud

BEEP — BEEEEEP!

I nearly jumped out of my fur, squeaking, "What was that?!"

I glanced around but didn't see anything unusual. My **BEDROOM** looked the same as it did every morning! Maybe it had only been a **nightmare** . . .

I had just pulled the covers over my snout again, when:

BEEP — BEEEEEP!

I immediately rushed downstairs, looked

out the window, and could not believe my eyes!

The Stilton **CHEESE-COLORED SUPERCAMPER** was parked on the street, right outside my door!

In the driver's seat, Grandfather William hollered through a **loudsqueaker**. "What are you doing in your pajamas, cheddarhead? We're leaving! **Move, move, move!**"

I was so surprised, I could barely squeak. "But I don't want to drive in that thing!"

My grandfather honked the horn for the third time.

BEEP — BEEEEEEP!

Then he bellowed, "Would you like me to use the smarty-mouse hook?"*

* See picture on pages 24 and 25.

Just then Thea stuck her snout out the supercamper's library window. "See, Geronimo? Grandfather William had a mouserific idea! We get to travel all together in the cheese-colored camper again. Remember when we traveled through Ratzikistan?"*

Squeak! Of course I remembered! I had NO intention of repeating that fur-raising experience.

The smarty-mouse hook suddenly came to life with a frightening metallic sound.

CREEEEAK!

Grandfather William squeaked at the top of his lungs, "Come on, Grandson! What are you waiting for?"

Tina Spicyfur, Grandfather William's

* Read all about it in my book *A Cheese-Colored Camper*.

SUPERCAMPER

It's not like other campers! This is a cheese-colored supercamper, equipped for almost anything! It can travel on the road like any other car, fly in the sky like an airplane, or sail on the water like a boat.

This is the smarty-mouse hook!
Let's go, let's go, let's go!
1011011

cook and housekeeper, appeared at the cheese-colored supercamper's dining room window. "Come on in, Geronimo. I made you breakfast!"

Grandfather William turned to Tina. "What else did you cook?"

Tina replied, "Nothing for you, Mr. William. Remember, you aren't a young mouse anymore!"

Grandfather started to squeak up and complain, but Tina waved her rolling pin. "You have to try to take better care of yourself! You can't survive on just sweets, croissants, and sugary cheese shakes. Understood?"

Then Tina turned to me. "What are you waiting for? Get your tail in gear, or your breakfast will get cold!"

I got ready in a heartbeat. I took off my pajamas, brushed my teeth, hopped in the shower, combed my whiskers, got dressed, and ten seconds later, I was sitting in the supercamper!

If there was one thing I couldn't say no to, it was Tina's cooking!

DESTINATION: FROZEN FUR PEAK

Tina served us breakfast in the huge dining room: mozzarella smoothies and toast with mascarpone and melted fontina.

Holey cheese, how delicious!

Grandfather William only had some RICOTTA YOGURT, which he ate in one bite. "I want something sweet!" he squeaked, but Tina's stern LOOK stopped him from saying anything else.

Thea asked, "So, Grandfather, where are we going?"

A smile crossed Grandfather

William's snout again. "We are heading to **Frozen Fur Peak**! We will sleep in the supercamper, surrounded by nature. It will be a truly **cool** road trip for the Stilton family!"

What? Frozen Fur Peak?!

I had been to that chilly place before, and I wasn't eager to go back!

Trappy excitedly pointed a paw to one of the pictures in the book I'd given her. "Look! Here's a **PICTURE** of the peak!"

SQUEAK! I was ready to twist my tail into knots!

The picture showed a sharp, dark peak, surrounded by a swirling **snowstorm**.

My whiskers were wobbling with fear just thinking about it!

I cleared my throat. "How about a different destination?"

Thea waved a paw dismissively. "What are you squeaking about, Geronimo? This will be a great opportunity for you to test out the snowshoes I gave you!"

Oh no! Cold and exercise? Unsqueakable! This didn't sound like my idea of fun at all.

Grandfather William headed up to the driver's seat. "Come on, Grandson! Help me with the map."

Why me?

"I'm going to take notes for my new article while we're driving," Thea said.

Grandfather William nodded with approval. "See that? Thea WORKS even on vacation! She is a real Stilton!"

Trap yawned. "I'm too tired! I can't keep my eyes open. I'm going to take a nap in the bedroom!"

Grandfather William nodded. "That's right, Trap! Vacation is for resting, too."

I cleared my throat. "B-but . . . to be honest . . ."

Benjamin grabbed my paw. "Uncle G, I would stay with you, but Trappy and I want to finish reading the books you gave us. Can we go to the library?"

"Of course you can!" Grandfather William said. "There is nothing as important as your **education**."

Tina squeaked up. "I'm going to the kitchen to get **LUNCH** ready. I have a mouthwatering menu in mind."

Rat-munching rattlesnakes, I was the only one left!

Grandfather William placed the **map** in my paws. "Hang on to this, and don't mess up. We have no time to lose! **Let's go, let's go, let's go!**"

I sat down in the passenger seat and unfolded the map, first **LEFT** to right, then **RIGHT** to left, then top to bottom, then bottom to top . . .

"This thing is enormouse!" I exclaimed.

Grandfather William pointed to a small spot on the map. "Look, this is New Mouse City." Then he pointed to another spot, all the way in the **north**. "And this is Frozen Fur Peak! Come on, **GIVE ME DIRECTIONS**! Our vacation is in your paws now."

Great Gouda! That's a lot of pressure.

With that, Grandfather William started up the supercamper. The Stilton family road trip had officially begun!

To the Left . . . or Maybe to the Right?

There was still something I didn't understand, so I cleared my throat. "Um, Grandfather? Why are you driving if the supercamper can **fly**?"

Grandfather William sighed. "Grandson, in the good old days, camper trips were taken on the road, so we'll do this trip the same way! **FOCUS** on the map now. Which way do we go?"

Rotten rat's teeth, I hadn't been paying attention!

We were close to the Rodent River. I held the enormouse map in my paws and said, "Hmm, I think we're here, so take the next

LEFT . . . oh, wait! Maybe RIGHT?"

"What did you say?" Grandfather William snapped. "Right or left?"

I hesitated. "Um . . . right, right!"

We took the right turn and ended up heading for a MOUNTAIN RANGE.

Grandfather William smiled. "Here are the mountains!" He drove ahead, full speed.

"Grandfather, I'm not totally sure this is the right way . . ." I squeaked under my breath.

"**WHAT DID YOU SAY?** Squeak up, Grandson!" my grandfather bellowed over the sound of the engine.

I waved a paw. "Nothing, nothing . . ."

We were driving up steep mountain **roads** now, each one more and more covered in **snow**.

Holey cheese, I had no idea where we were!

I peered at the map. Was this Mount Vamp? Roasted Rat Volcano?

I **turned** the map over and over in my paws. Finally, I had to admit it to myself.

We were lost!

Grandfather William glared at me. "Grandson, where are you taking us?"

"Well, to be honest," I said, "you were the one who —"

My grandfather's cheeks turned redder than the sauce on a double-cheese pizza.

"WHAT DID YOU SAY?"

Mousefully, just then we started heading downhill. Maybe we were almost out of that mountain **maze**! A mouse could dream, right?

A Stinky Lake

The fog had lifted, and we were driving alongside the bank of a quiet river.

"What river is this?" Grandfather William asked me. "I didn't know there were rivers in the north."

I checked the map. **Slimy Swiss balls**, where were we? Maybe we really were going the **wrong way**?

Squeak! If that was the case, Grandfather William wouldn't be happy at all!

Just then I spotted a **big body of water** on the horizon. I checked the map again. What a mousetastic relief! "We're almost there — that must be Brimstone Lake!"

We were heading **north** after all!

But at that moment, I got hit in the snout by a wave of something stinky, disgusting,

REVOLTING!

Grandfather William stopped the supercamper. "Rancid ricotta, what a smell!"

The rest of the family joined us in the front. Trappy and Benjamin were holding their snouts. "**Stinky, stinky, stinky!**"

Tina waved her rolling pin in dismay. "I can't even smell my cooking with all this **stink**!"

"What a horrible stench!" Trap exclaimed. "It smells like rotten **eggs**!"

"That's not rotten eggs," Thea explained. "It's sulfur. And that's not Brimstone Lake, it's the **Sulfurous Swamp**!"

"The Sulfurous Swamp?" I squeaked, feeling my tail start to tremble. "So . . ."

I checked the map again and immediately turned as **WHITE** as a ball of mozzarella cheese!

If this was the Sulfurous Swamp, it meant we were heading **South** . . . in the totally wrong direction!

Grandfather William grabbed the map from my paws. "I knew I shouldn't have trusted you, **cheesebrain**! We are going in the **COMPLETE** opposite direction from **FROZEN FUR PEAK**!"

Squeakkkk! Why, oh why, does everything always happen to me?

Thea stepped in to take control of the situation. "Since we're already here, how about we have a warm-weather vacation? It could be fabumouse!"

Grandfather William looked doubtful. "Here, at the Sulfurous Swamp? With this unbearable stench?"

Thea giggled. "No, Grandfather! The geysers aren't far from here. Their hot springs are known for their miraculous healing qualities. We could all use a few days to relax!"

Benjamin was holding his **BOOK** open to Mouse Island's warm vacation spots. "There is also a fancy spa with a famouse restaurant. The spa is called the Relaxing Rodent!"

Grandfather William sighed. "Okay, okay, you convinced me! After all, the best part of going on vacation in a **SUPERCAMPER** is that you can change your plans at any time."

PHEW! Maybe Grandfather would **forgive me** after all.

GEYSER

A geyser is a special kind of hot spring. Geysers are made from a tubelike hole in the Earth that is filled with water. The water inside is heated from below by molten rock called magma. Water near the bottom of the tube begins to boil and turns to steam. The steam jets toward the surface, pushing the water above with it.

These jets of hot water and steam can happen regularly, depending on the type of geyser, and can last from a few minutes to entire days. Some of the most famouse geysers in the world are located in Iceland. Others can be found in New Zealand, Alaska, Chile, Bolivia, Russia, and many other locations around the world. The most famouse geyser in the United States is Old Faithful, located in Yellowstone National Park.

Grandfather William turned to me. "Since this is your fault, you get to pay for us!"

Aaaargh! Why, oh why, does everything always happen to me?

Time to Kick Up Our Paws!

We left the Sulfurous Swamp (and its disgusting **stench**!) and headed toward the geysers.

Thea was in charge of the map now, and Grandfather William didn't miss a chance to **remind me of it**. "See, Geronimo? Thanks to your sister, we have arrived at the right place! Maybe I should have chosen her as editor of *The Rodent's Gazette* instead of you, **cheddarhead**!"

Why does Grandfather William take everything out on me?

After eating a mousetastic **lunch** prepared by Tina, we left the supercamper and walked over to the Relaxing Rodent Spa. It was an elegant building with a garden full of tropical flowers out front.

Upon seeing it, Trap exclaimed, "This looks like an EXPENSIVE place, Cousinkins! Since you're treating us, I think I'll get lots of mozzarella milkshakes to drink next to the pool." He grinned and raised his eyebrows at me.

RATS! My cousin will never change!

A very kind rodent welcomed us. "Hello! Would you like me to squeak to you about the services we offer?"

After listening to her tell us about all the relaxing activities we could take advantage of, Trap and Grandfather William decided to go to the sauna. Thea booked a relaxing massage.

Tina said, "What a fabumouse idea, Thea! I'll book a massage, too. Then I'll get some

The Relaxing Rodent

496 Geyser Street – Mouse Island

At the Relaxing Rodent Spa, we offer a variety of soothing treatments thanks to the nearby geysers and hot springs! Swim in our outdoor pool, featuring hydromassage.

After soaking in a warm bath, take a dip in our frozen fur pool. Then try a massage, or relax in the sauna or steam room!

For dinner, enjoy specialties from our world-renowned chef, Jean Tail Ratton, in welcoming surroundings!

The Relaxing Rodent Spa: Everything you need to relax!

snacks together for all of us."

Benjamin looked up at me. "Uncle G, will you go to the outdoor pool with us?"

"Mousetastic!" Trappy cheered. "Come on, it's right this way!"

I would rather have had a relaxing massage myself, but how could I say no to my dear little mouselets?

A moment later, I was standing next to the pool. That water looked chilly! I took a few steps and —

SWISHHH!

I slipped on a bar of soap that some rodent had dropped on the floor! Who in the world would leave that there?

I tried to stay on my paws, but . . .

WHAM!

Incredible!
Relaxing!
Help!
Nice and toasty!

Before I could squeak, I was flat on the ground.

"**OUCH!**" I yelped.

Trappy looked over at me and giggled. "Quit kidding around, Uncle G! Let's jump in!"

SPLASH!

She leaped into the water, followed by Benjamin.

"Come on, Uncle G!" Benjamin squeaked. "The water's **warm**!"

"Well, we just had lunch," I said. "Plus,

the water is deep, and I'm not an **ATHLETIC** rodent . . ."

Just then I noticed a smaller, shallow pool nearby. "Maybe I'll take a dip in there first."

I leaped into the water, but —

holey cheese!
It was freezing cold!

An employee softly explained, "Sir, this is the **FROZEN FUR** pool. It's good for your circulation!"

I sighed through chattering teeth. "I'll try the hydromassage."

But the water jets were so strong, they started tossing me **LEFT** and **RIGHT**! Double-twisted rattails . . . I felt like I was stuck in a blender!

I finally climbed out of the water and STAGGERED to a lounge chair. My head was spinning and I felt queasy. I thought I was supposed to be relaxing!

CHEESY CREAMPUFFS, THIS WAS GOING TERRIBLY!

Just then Trap walked by, holding a large mozzarella milkshake.

"What's going on, Cousinkins?" he asked. "You don't look relaxed at all! You should try a MEGA-EXTRA-MOZZARELLA-WOW milkshake! It's mousetastically expensive, but totally worth it. I've already had twenty of them!"

Rotten ricotta! How was I was supposed to pay for all those milkshakes?

Why, oh why,
does everything always
happen to me?

A Disastrous Dinner!

When it was time for dinner, we all went to the Relaxing Rodent's famouse **restaurant**. There was a candle on each table. The atmosphere was so nice and calm!

AH, AT LAST!

Tina tightened the ties on her apron. "Well, I'm headed to the kitchen!"

Grandfather William narrowed his eyes at her. "What do you mean? You can't cook here — there is an **award-winning** chef!"

She pointed a paw at him. "Sir, you are on a diet, remember? I will personally take care of your dinner."

Grandfather William frowned. "Can't I

TREAT myself on vacation?"

But Tina didn't budge. "No, no, and no! No one can keep me away from the kitchen!" She scurried off, holding her rolling pin in one paw.

After a few minutes, a very ANGRY chef stormed out. "That's my kitchen! How dare she! That really toasts my cheese!" He threw his hat on the floor and stomped away.

I turned as white as a slab of mozzarella. Squeak! What had we done?

Luckily, before long, the food was served: hot cheesy lasagna for everyone . . . and a CELERY STICK for Grandfather William!

Tina had prepared food for everyone in the restaurant!

Yum — the **LASAGNA** was absolutely delicious! I was feeling fabumousely relaxed now. Actually, I was getting sleepier and sleepier . . .

I **yawned**, stretched my paws above my head, and —

Oh no! I TRIPPED a waiter who was walking behind me! All the dishes he was carrying crashed to the floor and shattered.

What a mouserific mess!

The spa director rushed over. He pointed at me and squeaked, "You again! First you disrupt the pool area, then you stress out our chef, and now you DESTROY my china! Get out of here — now!"

Every rodent in the room was staring at me. Rats!

"Isn't that Geronimo Stilton, editor of *The Rodent's Gazette*?"

"Look at what he did — all those broken dishes!"

"That's right, it is him! And I thought he was a well-behaved rodent."

Isn't that
Geronimo Stilton?
Cheddarhead!
Hmm . . .
Get out!
What a
mouserific mes

"That guy is a real cheddarhead!"

I felt my fur turn red and my whiskers begin to wobble. To make things even worse, the manager had just put a very expensive bill in my paw!

Why, oh why,
does everything always
happen to me?

Up and Down the Sand Dunes

As we walked away from the spa, Thea tried to make me feel better. "Don't worry about it, Geronimo! Tonight we'll sleep in the supercamper, and tomorrow will be a marvemouse day."

I took a deep breath. My sister was right! It was useless to think about all the terrible things that had happened at the Relaxing Rodent.

When we got back to the supercamper, I slipped under the covers and fell fast asleep.

Finally, I could rest!

Until . . .

Ring!

I opened my eyes and peered outside. Unsqueakable — it was still dark!

Suddenly, Thea's voice rang out over the loudsqueaker. "Rise and shine, Stilton family! This morning, we will go watch the sunrise at the Mousehara Desert, just a few miles away!"

I could hear Trappy and Benjamin rejoicing next door. "HOORAY!"

I stumbled out of bed and found that Grandfather William was ready to go, sitting in the driver's seat. He started up the supercamper. "What a great idea, Thea. Let's go on an adventure!"

VROOOOOM!

Before long, we were motoring through the desert.

Incredimouse!
What a view!

How exciting—
we were going to
watch the sunrise
in the desert!

Watching the sun come up from behind the sand dunes was an incredimouse **experience**. Maybe Thea had been right to wake us up early!

At that moment, I heard my sister's voice over the loudsqueaker again. "Since we're already here, we might as well go **sandboarding**!"*

Sand . . . what? I couldn't understand a cheesecrumb of what she was talking about. "Thea, what do you mean?"

"It's a fun **SPORT**," she replied. "You slide down a sand dune standing on a special board!"

What?! **Slide down** the dune? Standing on a board? Cheese and crackers, I did not like that idea one bit!

I tried to come up with a good excuse. "But we don't have boards!"

* Sandboarding is similar to snowboarding, but instead of gliding on snow, you glide on sand.

Thea smiled. "Don't worry, Geronimo, I rented them, plus helmets, suits, and all the **GEAR** we need. Come on, let's go!"

"Have fun!" Tina said, waving a paw. "I'll have lunch ready when you get back."

We got off the supercamper, and Trap handed me a **board**. "This one's yours, Cousinkins. Looking forward to seeing you in action!"

Benjamin and Trappy both climbed to the top of a **DUNE** and rode the boards down on their bellies, laughing **happily** the whole way.

Thea turned to me. "Geronimo, you need to stand up on your board, like a professional."

Squeakkk! This looked scary enough as it was — after all, I'm kind of a 'fraidy mouse!

I tried sliding down the dune standing on my board, but I ended up rolling down like a ball of mozzarella! Oof!

Thea cheered me on. "Come on, try again! You can do it!"

I don't know how, but I managed to stand up and continue down the dune.

Suddenly, something strange happened . . .

VERY STRANGE!

The board slowly started to lift off the ground!

Crusty cat litter, help! What was going on?!

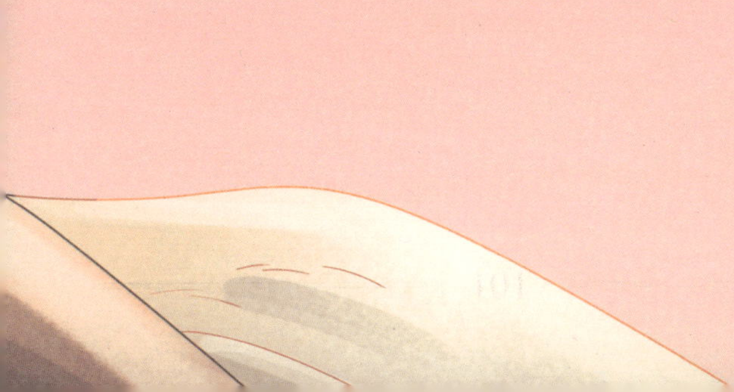

CAMELS ON THE RUN

The desert was getting farther and farther away from me!

Holey cheese, I was flying!

I held on to the board as tight as I could so I wouldn't fall. But — wait! At the **ENDS** of my board there were two **hot-air balloons**!

How did those get there?

Just then I heard Trap from **far below**, laughing and hollering, "Geronimo, how

do you like the automatic hot-air balloons I installed on your board? Fabumouse **prank**, right?"

Squeakkk! This wasn't fabumouse at all!

Before I could reply, a **GUST OF WIND**

pushed me even higher into the air. From above, the desert looked like an endless golden vista. I couldn't see the supercamper or my family anymore.

Yikes! Where was I? Where would I land? Oh, I'm too fond of my fur!

Right then the board started to lose altitude. The hot-air balloons deflated, and . . . **PFFFFF**!

I tumbled down to the sand, head over paws.

When I finally opened my eyes, I saw a big, furry **ANIMAL** snout very, very close to me.

I froze in my fur. What kind of animal was that?

I took a closer look.

It had:

✓an enormouse **nose**,

✓wide-set **EYES**, and

✓a tall **HUMP**.

Squeak! It was a camel!

And it was not alone. Cheesy creampuffs, I had tumbled into an enclosure with **THIRTEEN CAMELS**!

"At least they're peaceful animals," I told myself with a sigh.

But just then the camel closest to me **spit** right in my snout! Yuck!

All the other camels started spitting on me, too!

"**Help!**" I squeaked.

I started running, followed by the whole caravan of camels. Oh, what a mousely mess I'd gotten myself into!

I opened the **gate** of the enclosure in order to run as far away as possible, but the camels caught up with me. They passed right by me, **scattering** all over the desert.

Oh no! I had a bad feeling that I was in enormouse trouble!

THE OASIS OF THE SWEATY CAMEL

Suddenly, a rodent ran toward me, shouting: "Oh no! Oh no, no! Oh no, no, no!"

He looked at the enclosure, then mumbled hopelessly, "They really are all GONE."

"Oh, I'm so sorry!" I squeaked. "It was an accident!"

Just then more local rodents arrived.

One of them said, "The camels could be anywhere!"

Another exclaimed, "The desert is full of danger!"

A third added, "We have to get the village chief. This is an emergency!" Looking at me, he added, "Don't move. This is all your fault!"

Squeak! My WHISKERS wobbled with fear!

One rodent left, while the others stayed to make sure I didn't run off as fast as my paws would take me.

A few moments later, a stern-looking rodent arrived. He was taller than all the rest.

"My name is Amzar Mousin," he said to me. "I am the chief rodent of the Last Resort Oasis.

"For centuries, the residents of the oasis have looked after this rare breed of camel," he went on. "Now all of them have fled into the very dangerous Mousehara Desert! It's a disaster! A tragedy! A catastrophe!" He pointed a paw at me. "And **YOU** have to fix it!"

OH, I WAS REALLY UP TO MY SNOUT IN TROUBLE NOW!

The chief kept squeaking. "Our oasis will

not rest until all thirteen **spitting** camels are found!"

Suddenly, I heard a familiar voice. "Don't worry, **Amzar Mousin**, we will help you!"

I spun around — it was Grandfather William! Thea, Trap, Benjamin, Trappy, and Tina were all right on his tail.

Holey cheese, I was so happy to see them!

"Geronimo, when we saw you fly off, we ***RAN*** to the supercamper and started searching for you in the desert," Thea explained.

Benjamin threw his paws around me. "And here you are, Uncle G! I'm so glad we found you!"

Trap hung his snout. I could tell he was embarrassed about what he'd done. "I am so sorry, Cousinkins! The hot-air balloons were just a prank. I didn't mean to get you into such mousetastic **TROUBLE**!"

Well, what do you know? My cousin had a kind **heart** after all!

"Don't worry, Trap," I said. "What's important is that you're here now!"

Grandfather William clapped a paw on my shoulder. "**Grandson**, what trouble have you gotten yourself into this time?" He gave me a little smile. "I'm glad that you're all right. Now let's go find those **THIRTEEN CAMELS**!"

DESERT PRANKS

It was late morning, the sun was high in the sky, and the desert **heat** was unbearable. An egg-and-extra-cheese sandwich would have cooked on my snout in no time!

Benjamin looked down at his photography **BOOK**. "My book says that you need to have the appropriate **GEAR** to survive in the desert."

"Correct, Benjamin!" Thea replied. "I'll take care of that, since I've been to the desert **MANY** times before."

My sister walked back to the **SUPERCAMPER** to get everything we needed. In the twitch of a tail, she brought back:

- ✓sunglasses (since the sunlight was very bright),
- ✓compasses (to help us with directions in the dunes),
- ✓sun hats (since the sun was scorching our snouts),
- ✓wipes (to clean the sand out of our snouts and paws),
- ✓sunscreen (to protect our fur), and
- ✓eyedrops (to keep the wind from irritating our eyes).

"Now that we're ready, let's split into groups," Thea suggested.

"Split up?" I squeaked. "Is that really a good idea?"

Thea waved a paw. "Grandfather William and Tina will head NORTH, Trap and Benjamin will head SOUTH, Trappy and I will go WEST, and Geronimo will go EAST."

"Why do I have to go alone?" I complained.

Grandfather William rolled his eyes. "You caused this TROUBLE, Grandson! So don't complain."

Shrugging, I walked east, holding a compass. I climbed up and down the DUNES, but there was no sign of the camels!

The wind was blowing mousetastically hard — so hard that the compass fell out of my paws and TUMBLED AWAY!

For the love of cheese, how was I going to find my way now?

I looked around hopelessly . . . and saw the **SUPERCAMPER** on the horizon! Whew!

I tried walking toward it, but the more I moved my paws, the farther away the supercamper looked. Then it completely **disappeared**!

HOW STRANGE!

Suddenly, I saw palm trees. The **oasis**! I was safe!

I scurried toward it . . . but the oasis **disappeared**, too! Cheese and crackers!

HOW STRANGE!

I turned around, hanging my snout — and there was a camel. Holey cheese, it was one of the camels from the oasis!

I waved my paws. "Hey, wait up!"

But as I got closer, the camel disappeared, too!

HOW STRANGE!

What was going on?

It suddenly smacked me in the snout: These were only mirages!

And that meant I was LOST!

How was I going to FIND MY WAY back to the oasis?

I was trembling from snout to tail.

"HELLLLLLP!"

MIRAGE

A mirage is an optical illusion. It happens when rays of light pass through a layer of heated air of varying density. As they do, they turn into reflections. It becomes possible to see objects that look to be in one place when in reality they are in a completely different location.

Searching for the Lost Camels

Suddenly, I heard someone squeaking, "Mr. Stilton, is that you?"

I turned on my paws and saw Tina walking across the dunes, holding her rolling pin. Grandfather William was walking beside her. I happily ran toward her, but then I stopped cold. "Cheesy creampuffs, what if this is another mirage?" I squeaked to myself.

In response, Grandfather walked up and patted me on the shoulder. "What mirage? Are you feeling okay? We have already found and brought back three camels. What about you, cheddarhead. How many have you returned?"

I **whispered**, "Well, to be honest, I haven't found any yet."

Grandfather William's voice boomed in the desert. "Not even one? What are you waiting for? This used to be a vacation, but now there is work to do.

LET'S GO,
LET'S GO,
LET'S GOOOOO!"

"Look, Mr. Stilton," Tina said, pointing, "there's one right there!"

It was true! A CAMEL was sitting very comfortably on a nearby dune. I snuck closer, as quiet as a mouse, so I wouldn't scare it away. But, suddenly I felt a tickle in my nose . . .

ACHOO!

Oh no! My sneeze got the camel's attention. It spit on me and took off running!

I raced after the camel and was able to grab its REINS and hop onto its back. But unfortunately, it started RUNNING even faster!

I slipped, but my paw was stuck. Cheese

and crackers, the camel dragged me all the way back to the oasis!

Arghhhhhh!

My head hurt and I felt queasy, but at least I had managed to get one of the camels back! Well, I guess the camel brought me back, really.

The rest of the Stilton family was waiting at the oasis. They had gotten many of the camels back to the pen already. Only THREE were still missing!

Benjamin squeaked up. "Uncle G, I read in the book you gave me that camels love a local plant called DRINN."*

* Drinn's scientific name is *Aristida pungens*. It is a coarse, weedy grass that grows in the desert.

"We picked some, Gerrykins!" Trap added. "We were keeping busy while you were hopelessly trying to catch that one camel!"

I was at the end of my rope. "My name is Geronimoooooo!"

Trap slapped a paw on my shoulder. "Come on, Cousinkins, don't be so sensitive! Get the drinn, and let's go find the other camels."

I nodded and picked up a basket of DRINN. Then we headed back into the desert, all together. The sun was starting to go down. Holey cheese, we had to hurry!

Thea checked the compass. "Let's go southeast. Amzar Mousin told me that there is another small oasis in that direction.

Maybe the camels headed that way?"

Amzar Mousin was right! In the twitch of a tail, we spotted the three missing camels standing around, calmly drinking water from a small **pond** in the shade of a few palm trees.

Benjamin whispered, "Let's tiptoe so we don't **scare them away** . . ."

Just then the camels raised their

heads and **sniffed** something in the air.

The camels walked toward us, ***FASTER AND FASTER***. They were heading for . . . me!

"**Helpppp!**" I cried.

I started running as fast as my paws would take me, chased by those three **spitting** camels!

A PARTY IN THE OASIS

I was running, frightened, when Benjamin called, "Uncle G, remember that camels love DRINN! Get them to follow you all the way to the oasis!"

Holey cheese, my nephew was right! But I couldn't help being scared out of my fur. Those camels were REALLY FAST!

I tried to outrun them, while my family cheered me on.

"Let's go, let's go, let's go!" Grandfather William hollered.

"Come on, Geronimo!" Thea called. "This is your chance to get a little EXERCISE!"

I kept running, my tongue hanging out

of my mouth, until I spotted the oasis on the horizon.

Moldy mozzarella, I had made it!

When I reached the fence, I threw the basket of DRINN over and passed out on the ground.

To wake me up, Tina stuck a slice of **SMELLY CHEESE** under my snout.

Sniff . . . sniff . . .

After a few moments, I opened my eyes.

"Mr. Stilton, you were marvemouse!" Tina said. My whole family stood next to her, smiling.

Grandfather William said, "Mousetastic job this time, Grandson!"

In the meantime, the sun was going down behind the dunes, leaving a sky full of STARS above us.

What a fabumouse view!

Amzar Mousin walked over to us. "Dear Stilton family, thanks to you, the CAMELS are safe again," he said. "My friends and I would be honored to have you as our dinner guests. You can try all our most special dishes!"

"We'd love that, thank you," Grandfather William said. "I am tremendmousely hungry."

Tina narrowed her eyes at him. "Mr. William, I still need to approve all the meals you eat. They must be healthy foods!"

We followed Amzar Mousin over to a big fire. All the rodents were sitting close around it. Nights in the desert can be very **cold**!

We ate **couscous, vegetables, and soups**. Everything was mousetastic!

After dinner, we were served clove tea. Amzar Mousin announced, "Now I will tell you a desert **legend**."

Don't forget your diet!
Yum! Delicious!

Benjamin and Trappy cheered. "Ooh! How exciting!"

Sitting around the **FIRE**, we all listened to the deep, soothing voice of Amzar Mousin.

The Emerald-Horned Gazelle

Once upon a time, there was a caravan crossing the desert. The trip was long, and there was neither food nor water to be found. One day, a rodent from the caravan saw a **gazelle** with her fawns. He decided he would hunt the gazelles, for the rodents were all hungry for something other than dates and milk. His daughter, however, asked him to spare the fawn and her family, and he agreed.

A few days later, the **caravan** had very little water left, but they still had a long way to travel. During the night, the young mouselet who had saved the gazelle had a **dream**. She saw a gazelle with emerald horns who said, "Thank you for saving my life! I know your water supply is almost gone, but you have been so good to me." The gazelle knocked her head against the ground so that a small piece of her **emerald horn** broke off. "Take this, and when you have no more water, hold it tight."

When the mouselet woke up, she thought, *What a strange dream!* But when she put her paw in her pocket, she found a **green stone**! *Maybe it wasn't just a dream . . .*

The caravan started out again, and everyone was very worried. There was only one flask of water left.

That night, while everyone was asleep, the mouselet stepped out of her tent and held the green stone tight.

In no time, the emerald-horned **gazelle** appeared next to her. "Follow me!"

The mouselet walked beside her until the gazelle stopped right next to a heavy slab with a **ring** sticking out of the top.

The gazelle said, "Pull it!"

The mouselet didn't know how she would lift the slab on her own, but she trusted the gazelle.

As soon as she started pulling, she was surprised to see that she could lift the **stone slab** easily. But the biggest surprise was hearing a stream of water coming from below it!

The gazelle had led her to a **well**!

The mouselet had tears in her eyes. "Thank you — you have saved me and my family!"

The gazelle whispered, "Just as you did with me and my fawns."

The following day, the mouselet led the caravan to the well, where the rodents gratefully filled up their flasks with water.

Today, that mouselet is an older rodent who always wears a **necklace** with an emerald pendant, a precious reminder of her friend the gazelle!

On the Road Again

Amzar Mousin and the other oasis rodents were so **welcoming** that we decided to stay with them for a few more days.

The camel **mishap** was totally forgotten, and we had all become good friends! We spent our time there going for walks, singing, dancing, and telling stories around the fire. Someone was always playing beautiful music with an imzad. Benjamin and Trappy tried to learn to play a couple of songs.

IMZAD
The imzad is a small, single-string bowed instrument traditionally played by women.

Grandfather Shortpaws spent most of his time trying to eat unhealthy foods without getting caught. Tina always caught him! Thea took a million photos with her camera, and Trappy and Benjamin invented new games to play with the camels. It was truly fabumouse and relaxing!

Finally, it was time to leave. I walked by the camels' enclosure to say good-bye. They are actually quite cute, and it turned out, I might actually miss them. As I reached out to pet one of them, he turned to me and . . . spit!

He spit straight at my snout! Again!

Why, oh why, does everything always happen to me?

Trap **chuckled**. “I guess he really doesn’t like you, Cousinkins!”

I guess I was not going to miss those spitting **CAMELS** after all!

But I was sad to say good-bye to Amzar Mousin and the other rodents, now that they had all forgiven me.

I gave them my phone number, and I made sure they knew they had friends and a place to stay if they ever wanted to visit New Mouse City.

I was lost in my thoughts and memories of the trip, when suddenly . . .

BEEP-BEEEEEEP!

AAARGH!

I nearly jumped out of my fur!

Sitting in the driver's seat of the supercamper, Grandfather William shouted, "Come on, **cheddarhead**, get a move on! We're all waiting for you! You have to help me with the **map**. But this time, don't cause any more trouble!"

From the kitchen, Tina called, "Mr. Geronimo, your **breakfast** is ready for you: chocolate muffins and a mozzarella smoothie!"

In other words, the trip was back on! I wondered if we would head back to **New Mouse City** right away, or if we would stop somewhere else first.

The important thing was that I was with my family. Family, my dear rodents, is the safest and most marvemouse place in the whole world.

#30 The Mouse Island Marathon
#31 The Mysterious Cheese Thief
Christmas Catastrophe
#32 Valley of the Giant Skeletons
#33 Geronimo and the Gold Medal Mystery
#34 Geronimo Stilton, Secret Agent
#35 A Very Merry Christmas
#36 Geronimo's Valentine
#37 The Race Across America
#38 A Fabumouse School Adventure
#39 Singing Sensation
#40 The Karate Mouse
#41 Mighty Mount Kilimanjaro
#42 The Peculiar Pumpkin Thief
#43 I'm Not a Supermouse!
#44 The Giant Diamond Robbery
#45 Save the White Whale!
#46 The Haunted Castle
#47 Run for the Hills, Geronimo!
#48 The Mystery in Venice
#49 The Way of the Samurai
#50 This Hotel Is Haunted!
#51 The Enormouse Pearl Heist
#52 Mouse in Space!
#53 Rumble in the Jungle
#54 Get into Gear, Stilton!
#55 The Golden Statue Plot
#56 Flight of the Red Bandit
#57 The Stinky Cheese Vacation
#58 The Super Chef Contest
#59 Welcome to Moldy Manor
#60 The Treasure of Easter Island
#61 Mouse House Hunter
#62 Mouse Overboard!
#63 The Cheese Experiment
#64 Magical Mission
#65 Bollywood Burglary
#66 Operation: Secret Recipe
#67 The Chocolate Chase
#68 Cyber-Thief Showdown
#69 Hug a Tree, Geronimo
#70 The Phantom Bandit
#71 Geronimo on Ice!
#72 The Hawaiian Heist
#73 The Missing Movie
#74 Happy Birthday, Geronimo!
#75 The Sticky Situation
#76 Superstore Surprise
#77 The Last Resort Oasis

Up Next:

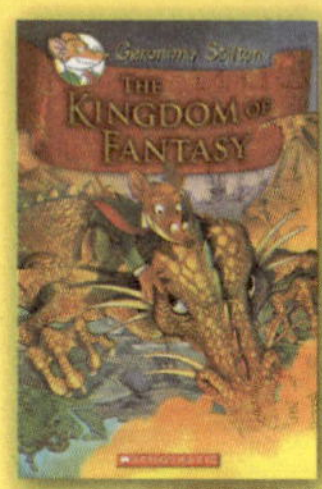

THE KINGDOM OF FANTASY

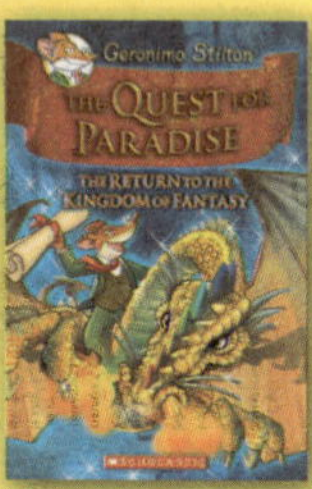

THE QUEST FOR PARADISE:
THE RETURN TO THE KINGDOM OF FANTASY

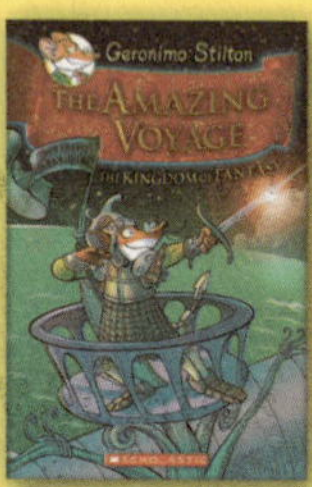

THE AMAZING VOYAGE:
THE THIRD ADVENTURE IN THE KINGDOM OF FANTASY

THE DRAGON PROPHECY:
THE FOURTH ADVENTURE IN THE KINGDOM OF FANTASY

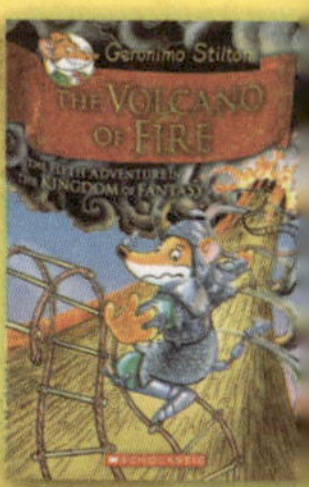

THE VOLCANO OF FIRE:
THE FIFTH ADVENTURE IN THE KINGDOM OF FANTASY

THE SEARCH FOR TREASURE:
THE SIXTH ADVENTURE IN THE KINGDOM OF FANTASY

THE ENCHANTED CHARMS:
THE SEVENTH ADVENTURE IN THE KINGDOM OF FANTASY

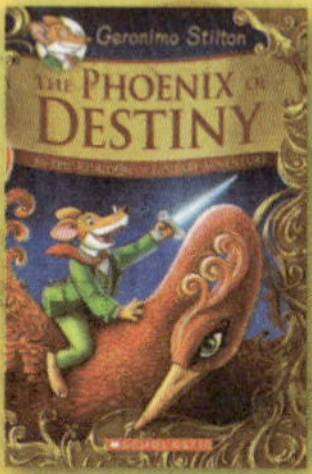

THE PHOENIX OF DESTINY:
AN EPIC KINGDOM OF FANTASY ADVENTURE

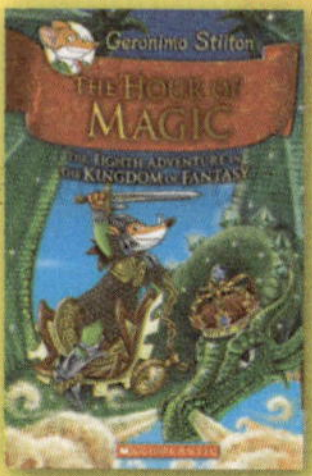

THE HOUR OF MAGIC:
THE EIGHTH ADVENTURE IN THE KINGDOM OF FANTASY

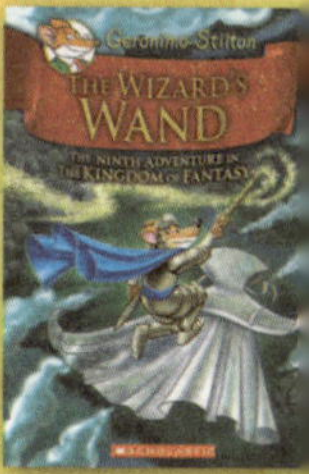

THE WIZARD'S WAND:
THE NINTH ADVENTUR IN THE KINGDOM OF FANTASY

THE SHIP OF SECRETS:
THE TENTH ADVENTURE IN THE KINGDOM OF FANTASY

THE DRAGON OF FORTUNE:
AN EPIC KINGDOM OF FANTASY ADVENTURE

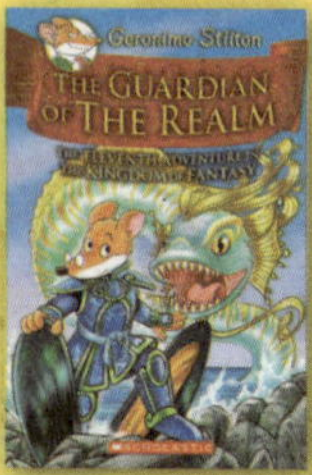

THE GUARDIAN OF THE REALM:
THE ELEVENTH ADVENTURE IN THE KINGDOM OF FANTASY

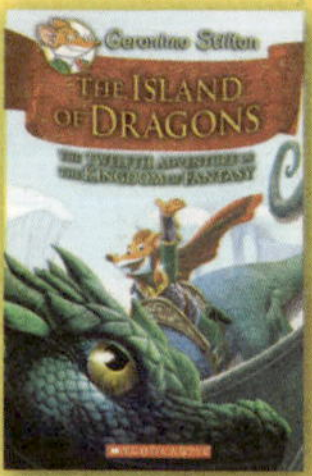

THE ISLAND OF DRAGONS:
THE TWELFTH ADVENTURE IN THE KINGDOM OF FANTASY

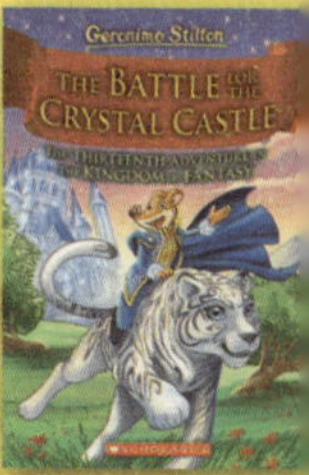

THE BATTLE FOR TH CRYSTAL CASTLE:
THE THIRTEENTH ADVENTU IN THE KINGDOM OF FANTASY

Visit Geronimo in every universe!

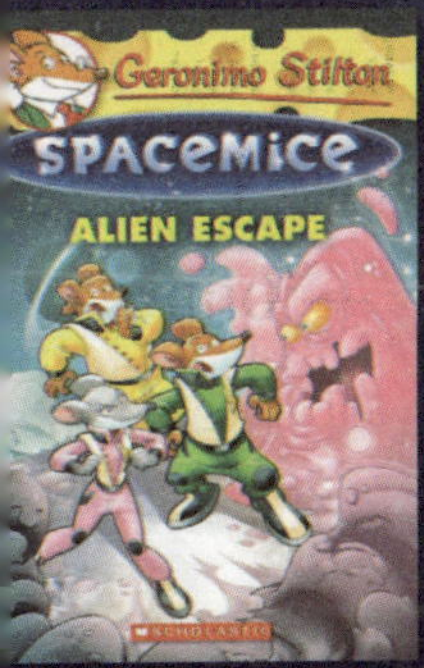

Spacemice

Geronimo Stiltonix and his crew are out of this world!

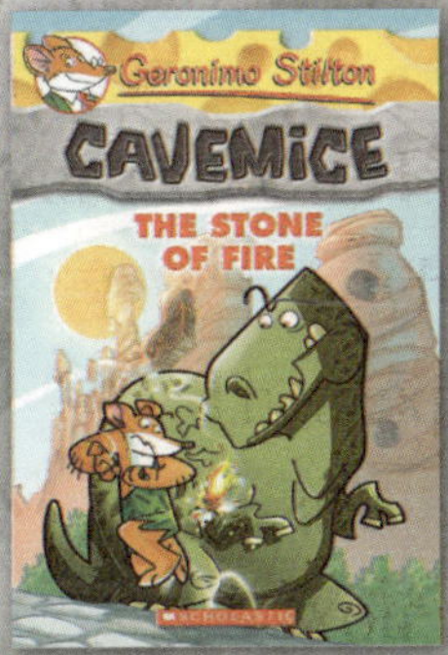

Cavemice

Geronimo Stiltonoot, an ancient ancestor, is friends with the dinosaurs in the Stone Age!

Micekings

Geronimo Stiltonord lives amongst the dragons in the ancient far north!

Don't miss any of these exciting Thea Sisters adventures!

Thea Stilton and the Dragon's Code

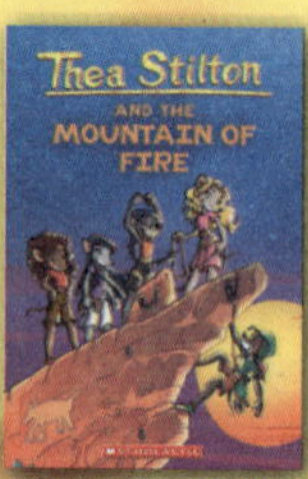

Thea Stilton and the Mountain of Fire

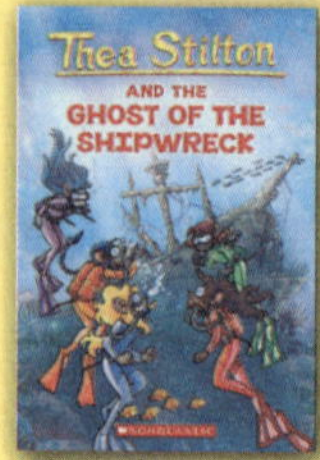

Thea Stilton and the Ghost of the Shipwreck

Thea Stilton and the Secret City

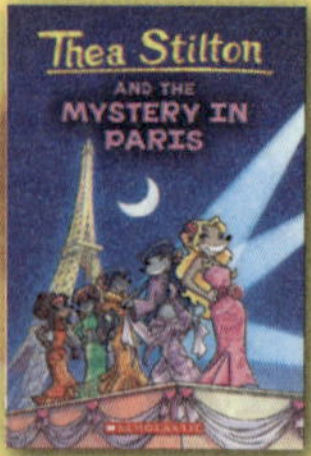

Thea Stilton and the Mystery in Paris

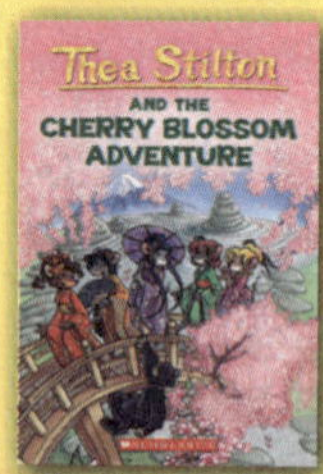

Thea Stilton and the Cherry Blossom Adventure

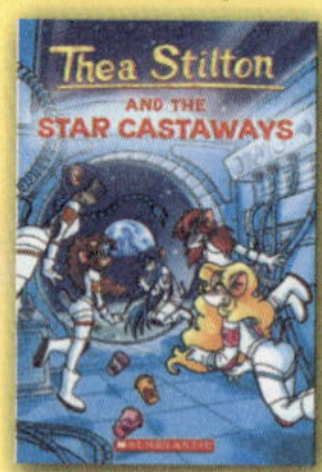

Thea Stilton and the Star Castaways

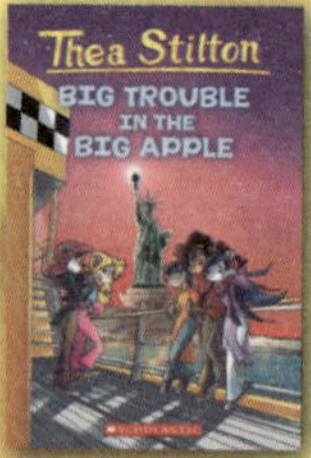

Thea Stilton: Big Trouble in the Big Apple

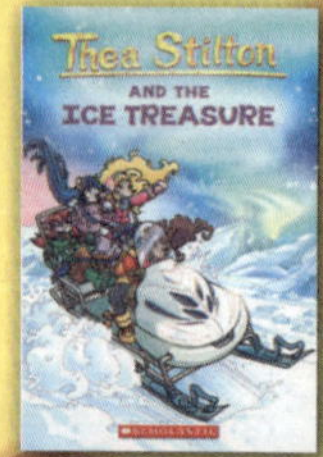

Thea Stilton and the Ice Treasure

Thea Stilton and the Secret of the Old Castle

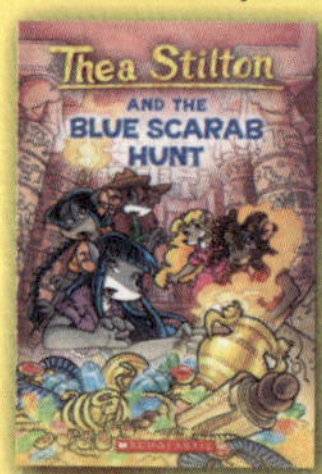

Thea Stilton and the Blue Scarab Hunt

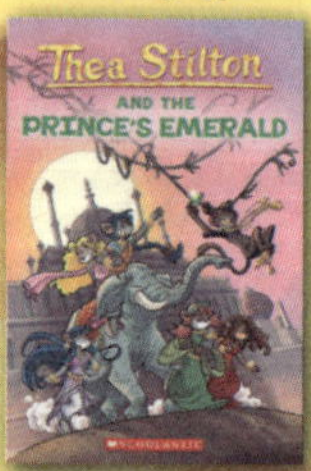

Thea Stilton and the Prince's Emerald

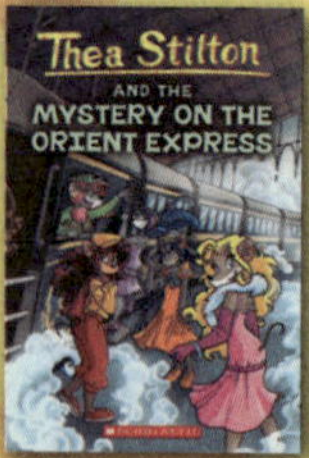

Thea Stilton and the Mystery on the Orient Express

Thea Stilton and the Dancing Shadows

Thea Stilton and the Legend of the Fire Flowers

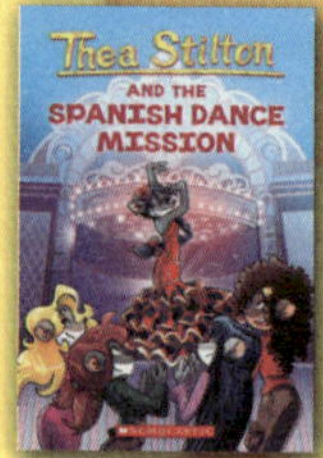

Thea Stilton and the Spanish Dance Mission

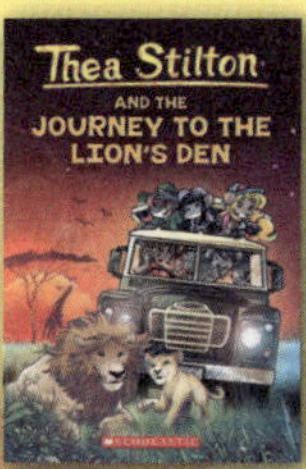

Thea Stilton and the Journey to the Lion's Den

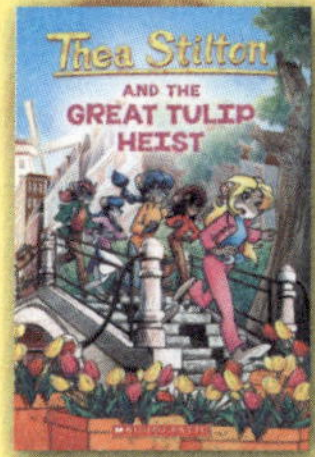

Thea Stilton and the Great Tulip Heist

Thea Stilton and the Chocolate Sabotage

Thea Stilton and the Missing Myth

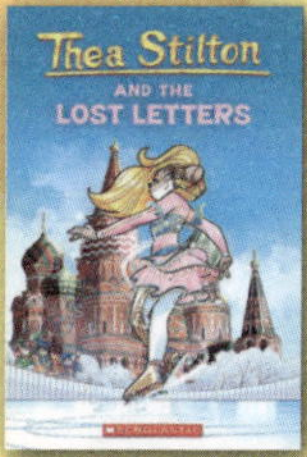

Thea Stilton and the Lost Letters

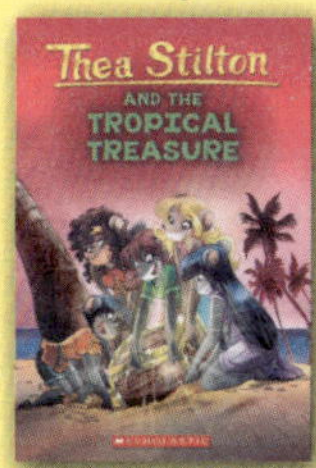

Thea Stilton and the Tropical Treasure

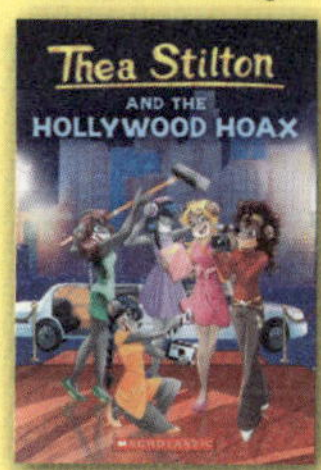

Thea Stilton and the Hollywood Hoax

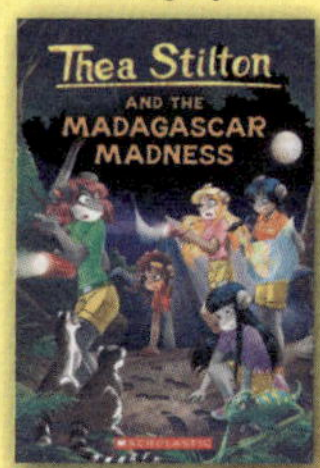

Thea Stilton and the Madagascar Madness

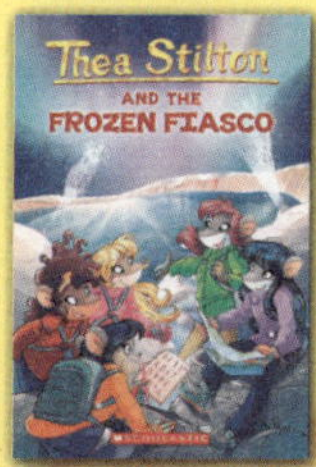

Thea Stilton and the Frozen Fiasco

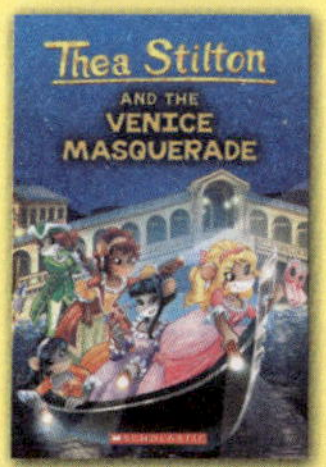

Thea Stilton and the Venice Masquerade

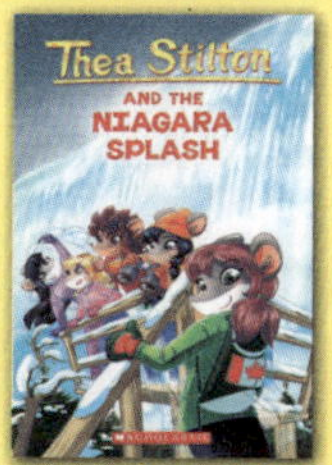

Thea Stilton and the Niagara Splash

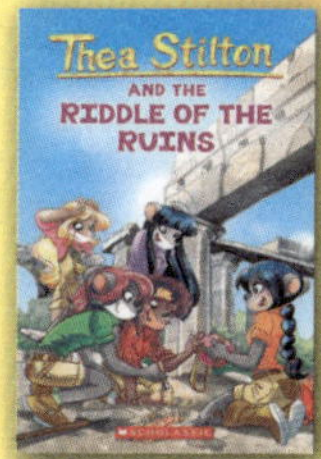

Thea Stilton and the Riddle of the Ruins

Thea Stilton and the Phantom of the Orchestra

Thea Stilton and the Black Forest Burglary

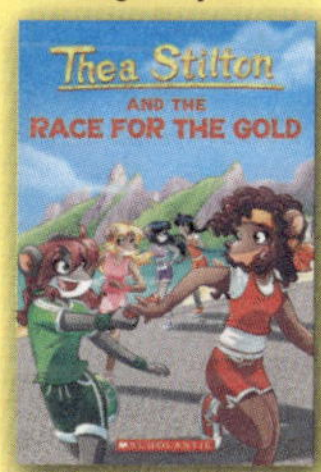

Thea Stilton and the Race for the Gold

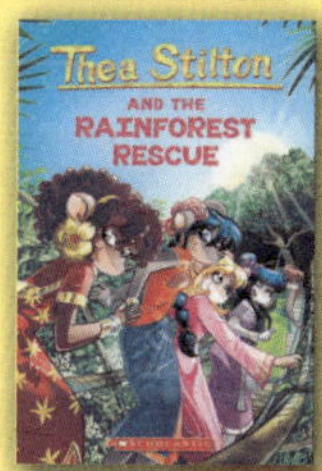

Thea Stilton and the Rainforest Rescue

Don't miss any of my fabumouse special editions!

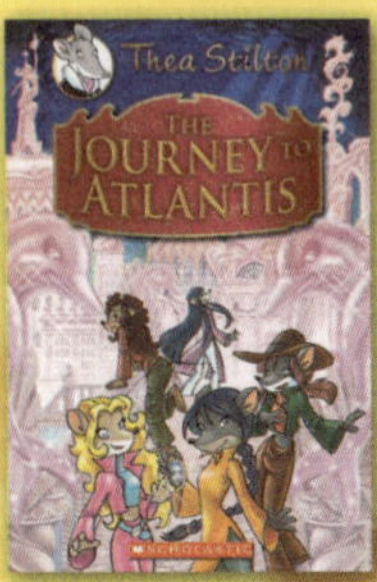

The Journey to Atlantis

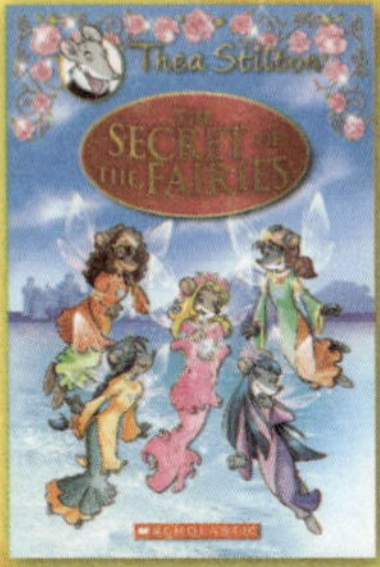

The Secret of the Fairies

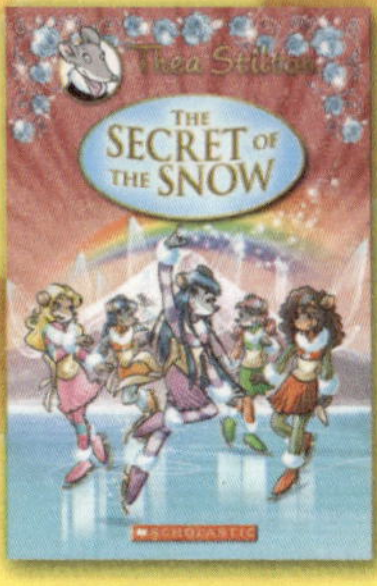

The Secret of the Snow

The Cloud Castle

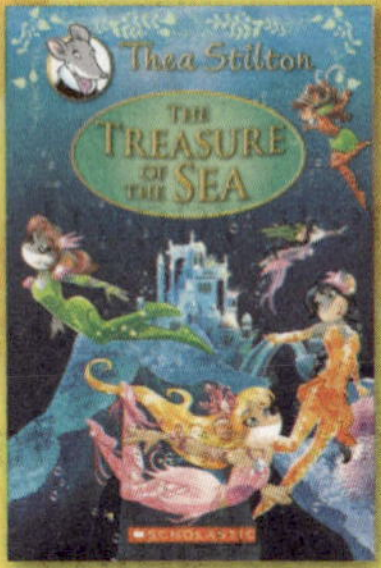

The Treasure of the Sea

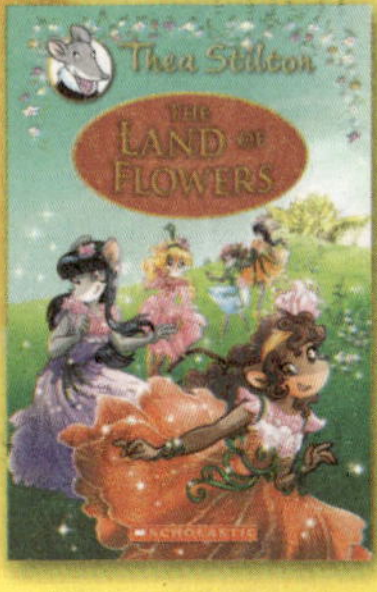

The Land of Flowers

The Secret of the Crystal Fairies

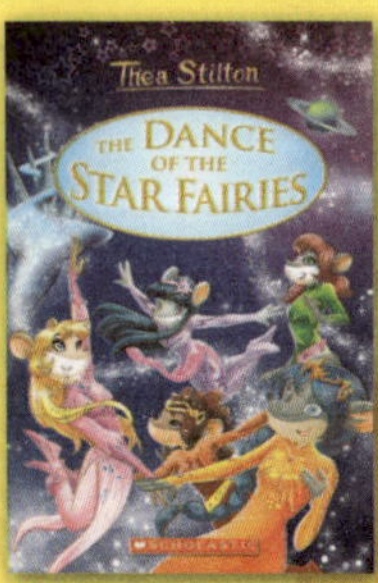

The Dance of the Star Fairies

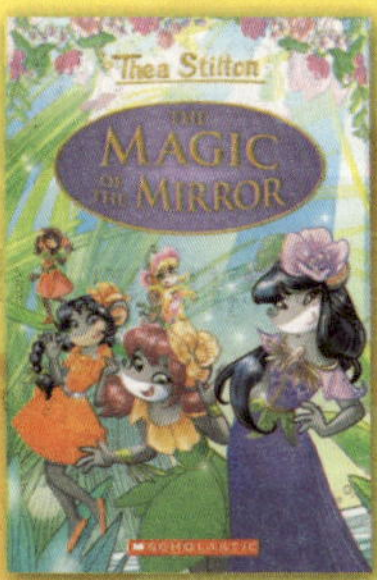

The Magic of the Mirror

Thea Stilton

Secret Fairies

Don't miss any of these exciting series featuring the Thea Sisters!

Treasure Seekers

Mouseford Academy

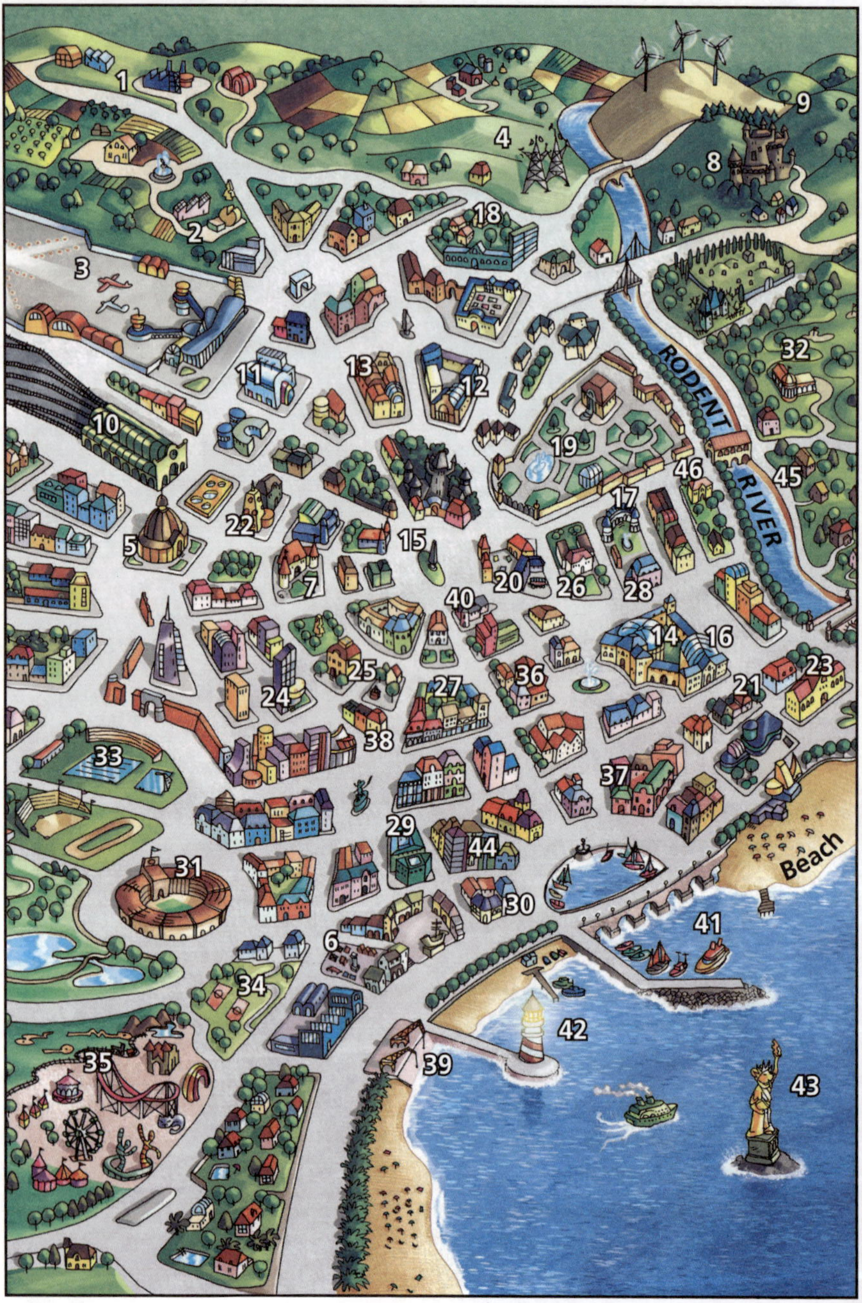
1
2
3
4
5
6
7
8
9
10
11
12
13
14
15
16
17
18
19
20
21
22
23
24
25
26
27
28
29
30
31
32
33
34
35
36
37
38
39
40
41
42
43
44
45
46
RODENT RIVER
Beach

Map of New Mouse City

1. Industrial Zone
2. Cheese Factories
3. Angorat International Airport
4. WRAT Radio and Television Station
5. Cheese Market
6. Fish Market
7. Town Hall
8. Snotnose Castle
9. The Seven Hills of Mouse Island
10. Mouse Central Station
11. Trade Center
12. Movie Theater
13. Gym
14. Catnegie Hall
15. Singing Stone Plaza
16. The Gouda Theater
17. Grand Hotel
18. Mouse General Hospital
19. Botanical Gardens
20. Cheap Junk for Less (Trap's store)
21. Aunt Sweetfur and Benjamin's House
22. Mouseum of Modern Art
23. University and Library
24. *The Daily Rat*
25. *The Rodent's Gazette*
26. Trap's House
27. Fashion District
28. The Mouse House Restaurant
29. Environmental Protection Center
30. Harbor Office
31. Mousidon Square Garden
32. Golf Course
33. Swimming Pool
34. Tennis Courts
35. Curlyfur Island Amousement Park
36. Geronimo's House
37. Historic District
38. Public Library
39. Shipyard
40. Thea's House
41. New Mouse Harbor
42. Luna Lighthouse
43. The Statue of Liberty
44. Hercule Poirat's Office
45. Petunia Pretty Paws's House
46. Grandfather William's House

This way to the Rodent Straits
Brigand's Isle
Pirate Ship of Cats
Tomcat Island
Cat's Claw Bay
Panther Archipelago
Hamster Islands
Blue Dolphin Bay
Swissville
Coral Reefs
This way to the Mousific Ocean
Stray Cat Harbor
Cheddarton
Mouseport
San Mouscisco
This way to the Ratlantic Ocean
New Mouse City
Mousefort Beach
Furflung Island
N
W
E
S
MOUSE ISLAND
This way to the Sea of Mice

Map of Mouse Island

1. Big Ice Lake
2. Frozen Fur Peak
3. Slipperyslopes Glacier
4. Coldcreeps Peak
5. Ratzikistan
6. Transratania
7. Mount Vamp
8. Roastedrat Volcano
9. Brimstone Lake
10. Poopedcat Pass
11. Stinko Peak
12. Dark Forest
13. Vain Vampires Valley
14. Goose Bumps Gorge
15. The Shadow Line Pass
16. Penny Pincher Castle
17. Nature Reserve Park
18. Las Ratayas Marinas
19. Fossil Forest
20. Lake Lake
21. Lake Lakelake
22. Lake Lakelakelake
23. Cheddar Crag
24. Cannycat Castle
25. Valley of the Giant Sequoia
26. Cheddar Springs
27. Sulfurous Swamp
28. Old Reliable Geyser
29. Vole Vale
30. Ravingrat Ravine
31. Gnat Marshes
32. Munster Highlands
33. Mousehara Desert
34. Oasis of the Sweaty Camel
35. Cabbagehead Hill
36. Rattytrap Jungle
37. Rio Mosquito

Dear mouse friends,
Thanks for reading, and farewell
till the next book.
It'll be another whisker-licking-good
adventure, and that's a promise!

Geronimo Stilton